50 Best Desserts in Town Recipes

By: Kelly Johnson

Table of Contents

- Chocolate Lava Cake
- Tiramisu
- Cheesecake
- Crème Brûlée
- Apple Pie
- Chocolate Mousse
- Vanilla Panna Cotta
- Baklava
- Lemon Meringue Pie
- Carrot Cake
- Red Velvet Cake
- Brownies
- Strawberry Shortcake
- Key Lime Pie
- Profiteroles
- Pecan Pie
- Eclairs
- Macarons
- Churros
- Rice Pudding
- Cannoli
- Peach Cobbler
- Chocolate Chip Cookies
- Baked Alaska
- Sorbet
- Pavlova
- Black Forest Cake
- S'mores
- Pudding Parfaits
- Gelato
- Coconut Cream Pie
- Mocha Cake
- Almond Joy Cake
- Chocolate Fudge Cake
- Banana Foster
- Sticky Toffee Pudding

- Fried Ice Cream
- Choco-Tacos
- Cheesecake Brownies
- Fruit Tart
- Milkshakes
- Tarte Tatin
- Cupcakes
- Lemon Bars
- Soufflé
- Almond Cake
- Strawberry Gelato
- Cinnamon Rolls
- Waffle Sundaes
- Nougat

Chocolate Lava Cake

Ingredients:

- 4 oz bittersweet chocolate
- 1/2 cup unsalted butter
- 1 cup powdered sugar
- 2 large eggs
- 2 large egg yolks
- 1/2 teaspoon vanilla extract
- 1/4 cup all-purpose flour
- Pinch of salt
- Butter and cocoa powder for greasing ramekins

Instructions:

1. Preheat the oven to 425°F (220°C). Grease four 6-ounce ramekins with butter and dust with cocoa powder.
2. In a heatproof bowl, melt the chocolate and butter together over a double boiler or in the microwave. Stir until smooth.
3. In another bowl, whisk the eggs, egg yolks, vanilla extract, and powdered sugar together until smooth.
4. Gradually add the melted chocolate mixture into the egg mixture, stirring to combine.
5. Fold in the flour and a pinch of salt.
6. Pour the batter into the prepared ramekins, filling each about 3/4 full.
7. Bake for 12-14 minutes, or until the edges are set but the center is still soft.
8. Let the cakes rest for 1 minute before carefully inverting them onto plates.
9. Serve immediately, dusted with powdered sugar or with vanilla ice cream.

Tiramisu

Ingredients:

- 1 1/2 cups heavy cream
- 1/2 cup mascarpone cheese
- 1/4 cup sugar
- 1 teaspoon vanilla extract
- 1 cup strong brewed coffee, cooled
- 1/4 cup coffee liqueur (optional)
- 2 packs of ladyfinger cookies
- Cocoa powder for dusting

Instructions:

1. In a mixing bowl, whisk together the heavy cream, mascarpone cheese, sugar, and vanilla extract until smooth and creamy.
2. In a shallow dish, combine the cooled coffee and coffee liqueur (if using).
3. Dip each ladyfinger into the coffee mixture for about 2 seconds, then layer them at the bottom of a serving dish.
4. Spread half of the mascarpone mixture over the ladyfingers.
5. Repeat with another layer of dipped ladyfingers and the remaining mascarpone mixture.
6. Cover and refrigerate for at least 4 hours, or overnight.
7. Just before serving, dust the top with cocoa powder.

Cheesecake

Ingredients:

- 2 cups graham cracker crumbs
- 1/4 cup sugar
- 1/2 cup unsalted butter, melted
- 4 packages (8 oz each) cream cheese, softened
- 1 cup sugar
- 1 teaspoon vanilla extract
- 4 large eggs
- 1 cup sour cream

Instructions:

1. Preheat the oven to 325°F (163°C). Grease a 9-inch springform pan.
2. In a bowl, mix the graham cracker crumbs, sugar, and melted butter. Press the mixture into the bottom of the prepared pan to form the crust.
3. In a separate bowl, beat the cream cheese and sugar until smooth. Add the vanilla extract and mix.
4. Add the eggs one at a time, mixing well after each addition.
5. Pour the cream cheese mixture over the crust in the springform pan.
6. Bake for 55-60 minutes, or until the center is set but slightly jiggly.
7. Remove from the oven and let cool. Once cooled, refrigerate for at least 4 hours or overnight.
8. Top with sour cream before serving.

Crème Brûlée

Ingredients:

- 2 cups heavy cream
- 1 vanilla bean, split and scraped (or 1 tablespoon vanilla extract)
- 5 large egg yolks
- 1/2 cup sugar
- 1/4 cup brown sugar (for caramelizing)

Instructions:

1. Preheat the oven to 325°F (163°C). Place four ramekins in a baking dish.
2. In a saucepan, heat the heavy cream and vanilla bean (or vanilla extract) over medium heat until hot but not boiling.
3. In a mixing bowl, whisk together the egg yolks and sugar until pale and thick.
4. Gradually pour the hot cream into the egg yolk mixture, whisking constantly.
5. Strain the mixture through a fine-mesh sieve into another bowl.
6. Pour the custard into the ramekins, dividing it evenly.
7. Fill the baking dish with hot water to come halfway up the sides of the ramekins.
8. Bake for 45-50 minutes, or until the custard is set but still jiggles slightly.
9. Let cool, then refrigerate for at least 2 hours.
10. Before serving, sprinkle brown sugar on top and caramelize with a kitchen torch.

Apple Pie

Ingredients:

- 6 cups sliced apples (Granny Smith or Honeycrisp)
- 1 tablespoon lemon juice
- 1 cup sugar
- 2 tablespoons all-purpose flour
- 1/2 teaspoon ground cinnamon
- 1/4 teaspoon ground nutmeg
- 1/4 teaspoon salt
- 2 tablespoons unsalted butter, cubed
- 1 package refrigerated pie crusts

Instructions:

1. Preheat the oven to 425°F (220°C).
2. In a large bowl, combine the sliced apples with lemon juice, sugar, flour, cinnamon, nutmeg, and salt.
3. Line a pie dish with one pie crust. Fill with the apple mixture and dot with butter.
4. Top with the second pie crust, sealing the edges. Cut slits in the top crust to allow steam to escape.
5. Bake for 45-50 minutes, or until the crust is golden brown and the filling is bubbling.
6. Let cool before serving.

Chocolate Mousse

Ingredients:

- 6 oz bittersweet chocolate, chopped
- 1 cup heavy cream
- 2 large eggs, separated
- 1/4 cup sugar
- 1 teaspoon vanilla extract

Instructions:

1. In a heatproof bowl, melt the chocolate over a double boiler or in the microwave. Let cool.
2. In a separate bowl, beat the egg yolks and sugar until thick and pale. Stir in the melted chocolate and vanilla extract.
3. Whip the heavy cream until soft peaks form, then fold into the chocolate mixture.
4. Beat the egg whites until stiff peaks form, then fold them into the mixture.
5. Spoon the mousse into individual cups and refrigerate for at least 2 hours before serving.

Vanilla Panna Cotta

Ingredients:

- 2 cups heavy cream
- 1 cup milk
- 1/2 cup sugar
- 1 vanilla bean, split and scraped (or 1 tablespoon vanilla extract)
- 2 teaspoons gelatin powder
- 3 tablespoons water

Instructions:

1. In a saucepan, heat the cream, milk, and sugar over medium heat. Add the vanilla bean and seeds, and simmer for 5 minutes.
2. In a small bowl, dissolve the gelatin in water and let it bloom for 5 minutes.
3. Remove the cream mixture from heat and stir in the gelatin until dissolved.
4. Pour the mixture into individual cups and refrigerate for at least 4 hours.
5. Serve chilled with fresh berries or fruit compote.

Baklava

Ingredients:

- 1 package phyllo dough
- 2 cups mixed nuts (pistachios, walnuts, almonds), chopped
- 1 teaspoon ground cinnamon
- 1 cup butter, melted
- 1 cup sugar
- 1/2 cup water
- 1/2 cup honey
- 1 tablespoon lemon juice

Instructions:

1. Preheat the oven to 350°F (175°C).
2. Layer 8-10 sheets of phyllo dough in a baking dish, brushing each sheet with melted butter.
3. Sprinkle a thin layer of nuts and cinnamon on top of the phyllo dough.
4. Continue layering phyllo dough, butter, and nuts until all the ingredients are used.
5. Cut the baklava into diamond shapes.
6. Bake for 45-50 minutes, or until golden brown and crisp.
7. In a saucepan, combine sugar, water, honey, and lemon juice. Bring to a simmer and cook for 10 minutes.
8. Pour the hot syrup over the baked baklava and let it soak for several hours before serving.

Lemon Meringue Pie

Ingredients:

- 1 pie crust, pre-baked
- 1 cup sugar
- 2 tablespoons cornstarch
- 1/4 teaspoon salt
- 1 1/2 cups water
- 3 large egg yolks
- 1/4 cup fresh lemon juice
- 2 tablespoons unsalted butter
- 3 large egg whites
- 1/4 teaspoon cream of tartar
- 1/4 cup sugar

Instructions:

1. Preheat the oven to 350°F (175°C).
2. In a saucepan, combine sugar, cornstarch, and salt. Gradually add water and cook over medium heat until thickened.
3. In a separate bowl, whisk the egg yolks, then slowly temper them by adding a bit of the hot sugar mixture. Return the egg yolk mixture to the saucepan.
4. Stir in lemon juice and butter, then pour the filling into the pre-baked pie crust.
5. In a mixing bowl, beat the egg whites with cream of tartar until soft peaks form. Gradually add sugar and beat until stiff peaks form.
6. Spread the meringue over the pie, making sure it touches the crust edges to prevent shrinking.
7. Bake for 10-12 minutes, or until golden brown. Cool completely before serving.

Carrot Cake

Ingredients:

- 2 cups all-purpose flour
- 2 teaspoons baking powder
- 1/2 teaspoon baking soda
- 1/2 teaspoon salt
- 1 1/2 teaspoons ground cinnamon
- 1/2 teaspoon ground nutmeg
- 1/2 cup vegetable oil
- 1 cup sugar
- 4 large eggs
- 2 teaspoons vanilla extract
- 2 cups grated carrots
- 1/2 cup chopped walnuts (optional)

Instructions:

1. Preheat the oven to 350°F (175°C). Grease and flour two 9-inch round cake pans.
2. In a bowl, combine the flour, baking powder, baking soda, salt, cinnamon, and nutmeg.
3. In another bowl, beat together the oil, sugar, eggs, and vanilla extract.
4. Gradually add the dry ingredients to the wet ingredients, mixing until just combined.
5. Fold in the grated carrots and walnuts.
6. Divide the batter evenly between the cake pans.
7. Bake for 30-35 minutes, or until a toothpick inserted into the center comes out clean.
8. Let the cakes cool, then frost with cream cheese frosting before serving.

Red Velvet Cake

Ingredients:

- 2 1/2 cups all-purpose flour
- 1 1/2 cups sugar
- 1 teaspoon baking soda
- 1 teaspoon cocoa powder
- 1 teaspoon salt
- 1 1/2 cups vegetable oil
- 1 cup buttermilk
- 2 large eggs
- 2 tablespoons red food coloring
- 1 teaspoon vanilla extract
- 1 teaspoon white vinegar
- Cream cheese frosting (recipe below)

Instructions:

1. Preheat the oven to 350°F (175°C). Grease and flour two 9-inch round cake pans.
2. In a large bowl, whisk together flour, sugar, baking soda, cocoa powder, and salt.
3. In a separate bowl, mix oil, buttermilk, eggs, food coloring, vanilla extract, and vinegar.
4. Gradually add the wet ingredients to the dry ingredients, mixing until smooth.
5. Divide the batter evenly between the two pans.
6. Bake for 25-30 minutes, or until a toothpick inserted comes out clean.
7. Let the cakes cool before frosting with cream cheese frosting.

Cream Cheese Frosting:

- 8 oz cream cheese, softened
- 1/2 cup unsalted butter, softened
- 4 cups powdered sugar
- 1 teaspoon vanilla extract

Instructions for Frosting:

1. Beat the cream cheese and butter until smooth.
2. Gradually add powdered sugar and vanilla extract, beating until fluffy.
3. Frost the cooled cakes and serve.

Brownies

Ingredients:

- 1 cup unsalted butter
- 8 oz bittersweet chocolate, chopped
- 1 1/4 cups sugar
- 3 large eggs
- 1 teaspoon vanilla extract
- 1/2 cup all-purpose flour
- 1/4 teaspoon salt

Instructions:

1. Preheat the oven to 350°F (175°C). Grease and flour a 9x9-inch baking pan.
2. In a saucepan, melt the butter and chopped chocolate over low heat, stirring constantly until smooth.
3. Remove from heat and whisk in sugar, eggs, and vanilla extract.
4. Stir in the flour and salt until combined.
5. Pour the batter into the prepared pan and bake for 20-25 minutes, or until a toothpick comes out with a few moist crumbs.
6. Let cool before cutting into squares.

Strawberry Shortcake

Ingredients:

- 4 cups fresh strawberries, sliced
- 1/4 cup sugar
- 2 cups all-purpose flour
- 2 teaspoons baking powder
- 1/2 teaspoon salt
- 1/4 cup sugar
- 1/2 cup unsalted butter, cubed
- 1 cup heavy cream
- Whipped cream for topping

Instructions:

1. In a bowl, combine strawberries and sugar. Let sit for 30 minutes to macerate.
2. Preheat the oven to 425°F (220°C). In a bowl, whisk together flour, baking powder, salt, and sugar.
3. Cut in the butter until the mixture resembles coarse crumbs. Add the heavy cream and stir until just combined.
4. Turn the dough out onto a floured surface, knead lightly, and roll out to about 1-inch thickness.
5. Cut into rounds and place on a baking sheet. Bake for 12-15 minutes, or until golden brown.
6. Assemble by splitting the shortcakes in half, adding strawberries and whipped cream in the middle, and topping with more strawberries.

Key Lime Pie

Ingredients:

- 1 1/2 cups graham cracker crumbs
- 1/4 cup sugar
- 1/2 cup unsalted butter, melted
- 3 large egg yolks
- 1 can (14 oz) sweetened condensed milk
- 1/2 cup fresh key lime juice
- 1 tablespoon lime zest
- Whipped cream for topping

Instructions:

1. Preheat the oven to 350°F (175°C). In a bowl, mix the graham cracker crumbs, sugar, and melted butter.
2. Press the mixture into the bottom of a pie pan and bake for 10 minutes.
3. In a bowl, whisk together egg yolks, sweetened condensed milk, lime juice, and lime zest.
4. Pour the filling into the baked crust and bake for 15 minutes.
5. Let the pie cool, then refrigerate for at least 2 hours before serving.
6. Top with whipped cream before serving.

Profiteroles

Ingredients:

- 1 cup water
- 1/2 cup unsalted butter
- 1 cup all-purpose flour
- 1/4 teaspoon salt
- 4 large eggs
- 1/2 cup whipped cream
- 1/4 cup chocolate ganache (optional)

Instructions:

1. Preheat the oven to 425°F (220°C). Line a baking sheet with parchment paper.
2. In a saucepan, bring water and butter to a boil. Remove from heat and stir in flour and salt until smooth.
3. Add eggs one at a time, beating after each addition until smooth.
4. Drop spoonfuls of dough onto the prepared baking sheet.
5. Bake for 20-25 minutes, or until golden brown and puffed.
6. Once cooled, fill with whipped cream and drizzle with chocolate ganache, if desired.

Pecan Pie

Ingredients:

- 1 1/2 cups pecan halves
- 3/4 cup corn syrup
- 3/4 cup brown sugar
- 1/4 cup unsalted butter, melted
- 3 large eggs
- 1 teaspoon vanilla extract
- 1/4 teaspoon salt
- 1 pie crust, pre-baked

Instructions:

1. Preheat the oven to 350°F (175°C). Arrange the pecans in the pie crust.
2. In a bowl, whisk together corn syrup, brown sugar, melted butter, eggs, vanilla extract, and salt.
3. Pour the mixture over the pecans.
4. Bake for 45-50 minutes, or until the filling is set.
5. Let cool before serving.

Eclairs

Ingredients:

- 1/2 cup unsalted butter
- 1 cup water
- 1 cup all-purpose flour
- 4 large eggs
- 1 cup heavy cream
- 1/4 cup powdered sugar
- 6 oz bittersweet chocolate, chopped

Instructions:

1. Preheat the oven to 400°F (200°C). Line a baking sheet with parchment paper.
2. In a saucepan, combine butter and water and bring to a boil. Stir in flour and cook for 1-2 minutes.
3. Remove from heat and add eggs one at a time, mixing after each addition.
4. Pipe the dough onto the prepared baking sheet in long strips.
5. Bake for 25-30 minutes, or until golden brown.
6. Let the eclairs cool.
7. In a bowl, whip the heavy cream and powdered sugar until stiff peaks form. Fill the eclairs with whipped cream.
8. Melt the chocolate and drizzle over the eclairs.

Macarons

Ingredients:

- 1 3/4 cups powdered sugar
- 1 cup almond flour
- 3 large egg whites
- 1/4 cup granulated sugar
- 1 teaspoon vanilla extract
- Buttercream filling (recipe below)

Instructions:

1. Preheat the oven to 300°F (150°C). Line a baking sheet with parchment paper.
2. Sift powdered sugar and almond flour together in a bowl.
3. In a separate bowl, beat egg whites until stiff peaks form, gradually adding granulated sugar.
4. Gently fold the almond mixture into the egg whites until smooth.
5. Pipe the batter into small circles on the prepared baking sheet.
6. Let the macarons sit at room temperature for 30 minutes to form a skin.
7. Bake for 15-20 minutes, or until the shells are firm and do not stick to the paper.
8. Once cooled, sandwich with buttercream filling.

Buttercream Filling:

- 1/2 cup unsalted butter, softened
- 1 cup powdered sugar
- 1 teaspoon vanilla extract

Instructions for Filling:

1. Beat butter until creamy.
2. Gradually add powdered sugar and vanilla extract until smooth.

Churros

Ingredients:

- 1 cup water
- 1/4 cup unsalted butter
- 1 tablespoon sugar
- 1/4 teaspoon salt
- 1 cup all-purpose flour
- 2 large eggs
- Cinnamon sugar for coating

Instructions:

1. In a saucepan, bring water, butter, sugar, and salt to a boil.
2. Stir in flour and cook for 1-2 minutes until a dough forms.
3. Remove from heat and stir in eggs one at a time until smooth.
4. Heat oil in a frying pan to 350°F (175°C).
5. Pipe the dough into the hot oil and fry until golden brown.
6. Remove from oil and coat with cinnamon sugar.

Rice Pudding

Ingredients:

- 1 cup Arborio rice
- 4 cups milk
- 1/2 cup sugar
- 1 teaspoon vanilla extract
- 1/2 teaspoon ground cinnamon

Instructions:

1. In a saucepan, combine rice, milk, and sugar. Cook over medium heat, stirring frequently, until the rice is tender and the pudding thickens.
2. Remove from heat and stir in vanilla extract and cinnamon.
3. Serve warm or chilled.

Cannoli

Ingredients:

- 12 cannoli shells (store-bought or homemade)
- 2 cups ricotta cheese, drained
- 1 cup powdered sugar
- 1 teaspoon vanilla extract
- 1/2 cup mini chocolate chips
- Chopped pistachios for garnish (optional)

Instructions:

1. In a bowl, mix ricotta cheese, powdered sugar, and vanilla extract until smooth.
2. Fold in the mini chocolate chips.
3. Fill the cannoli shells with the ricotta mixture.
4. Garnish with chopped pistachios or additional chocolate chips.
5. Serve immediately.

Peach Cobbler

Ingredients:

- 6 cups fresh or frozen peaches, sliced
- 1/2 cup sugar
- 1 tablespoon lemon juice
- 1 teaspoon vanilla extract
- 1 tablespoon cornstarch
- 1 cup all-purpose flour
- 1 teaspoon baking powder
- 1/4 teaspoon salt
- 1/2 cup unsalted butter, melted
- 1/4 cup milk
- 1/2 cup sugar (for topping)
- 1 teaspoon cinnamon

Instructions:

1. Preheat the oven to 375°F (190°C). Grease a 9x13-inch baking dish.
2. In a bowl, toss peaches with 1/2 cup sugar, lemon juice, vanilla extract, and cornstarch. Pour into the prepared baking dish.
3. In a separate bowl, mix together flour, baking powder, salt, melted butter, and milk to form a dough.
4. Spoon the dough over the peaches.
5. Sprinkle the top with 1/2 cup sugar and cinnamon.
6. Bake for 35-40 minutes, or until the topping is golden and the peaches are bubbly.
7. Serve warm with vanilla ice cream or whipped cream.

Chocolate Chip Cookies

Ingredients:

- 2 1/4 cups all-purpose flour
- 1 teaspoon baking soda
- 1/2 teaspoon salt
- 1 cup unsalted butter, softened
- 3/4 cup granulated sugar
- 3/4 cup packed brown sugar
- 1 teaspoon vanilla extract
- 2 large eggs
- 2 cups semisweet chocolate chips

Instructions:

1. Preheat the oven to 350°F (175°C). Line a baking sheet with parchment paper.
2. In a bowl, whisk together flour, baking soda, and salt.
3. In a large bowl, cream together butter, granulated sugar, brown sugar, and vanilla extract until smooth.
4. Beat in the eggs one at a time.
5. Gradually add the flour mixture and mix until combined.
6. Fold in the chocolate chips.
7. Drop spoonfuls of dough onto the prepared baking sheet, spacing them about 2 inches apart.
8. Bake for 10-12 minutes, or until golden brown.
9. Cool on the baking sheet for a few minutes before transferring to a wire rack.

Baked Alaska

Ingredients:

- 1 pint vanilla ice cream
- 1 pint chocolate ice cream
- 1 sponge cake or pound cake, sliced
- 4 large egg whites
- 1/2 cup granulated sugar
- 1/4 teaspoon cream of tartar

Instructions:

1. Line a bowl with plastic wrap and place a layer of vanilla ice cream, then chocolate ice cream on top. Freeze until firm.
2. Slice the cake and arrange the slices around the ice cream to form a "base."
3. Beat egg whites with sugar and cream of tartar until stiff peaks form.
4. Preheat the oven to 500°F (260°C). Place the ice cream and cake on a baking sheet.
5. Spread the meringue over the entire dessert, covering it completely.
6. Bake for 3-5 minutes or until the meringue is golden.
7. Serve immediately.

Sorbet

Ingredients:

- 4 cups fruit puree (such as mango, raspberry, or lemon)
- 1 cup sugar
- 1/2 cup water
- 1 tablespoon lemon juice (optional)

Instructions:

1. In a saucepan, combine sugar and water. Heat until the sugar dissolves, then let cool.
2. Mix the fruit puree, lemon juice (if using), and cooled sugar syrup.
3. Pour the mixture into an ice cream maker and churn according to the manufacturer's instructions.
4. Transfer the sorbet to an airtight container and freeze for at least 4 hours before serving.

Pavlova

Ingredients:

- 4 large egg whites
- 1 cup granulated sugar
- 1 teaspoon vanilla extract
- 1 teaspoon white vinegar
- 2 teaspoons cornstarch
- Fresh fruits for topping (berries, kiwi, passion fruit)

Instructions:

1. Preheat the oven to 250°F (120°C). Line a baking sheet with parchment paper.
2. Beat egg whites until soft peaks form. Gradually add sugar, a tablespoon at a time, until stiff peaks form.
3. Add vanilla extract, vinegar, and cornstarch. Fold gently.
4. Spoon the meringue onto the baking sheet, shaping it into a round disk with a slight well in the center.
5. Bake for 1 hour, then turn off the oven and let the pavlova cool completely in the oven.
6. Top with fresh fruits and serve immediately.

Black Forest Cake

Ingredients:

- 2 cups all-purpose flour
- 1 1/2 teaspoons baking powder
- 1/2 teaspoon baking soda
- 1/4 teaspoon salt
- 1/2 cup unsweetened cocoa powder
- 1 1/2 cups sugar
- 1/2 cup unsalted butter, softened
- 2 large eggs
- 1 teaspoon vanilla extract
- 1 cup buttermilk
- 1 jar (14 oz) morello cherries, drained, juice reserved
- 2 cups heavy cream, whipped
- 1/4 cup powdered sugar

Instructions:

1. Preheat the oven to 350°F (175°C). Grease and flour two 9-inch round cake pans.
2. In a bowl, mix flour, cocoa powder, baking powder, baking soda, and salt.
3. In a separate bowl, beat sugar and butter until creamy. Add eggs one at a time, then add vanilla extract.
4. Add the dry ingredients alternately with the buttermilk, mixing until smooth.
5. Pour the batter into the cake pans and bake for 30-35 minutes, or until a toothpick comes out clean.
6. Cool completely before assembling.
7. Slice the cakes in half and layer with whipped cream and cherries. Repeat the layers and top with whipped cream and chocolate shavings.

S'mores

Ingredients:

- Graham crackers
- Marshmallows
- Chocolate bars (milk or dark)

Instructions:

1. Toast marshmallows over an open flame until golden and gooey.
2. Break graham crackers into squares. Place a piece of chocolate on one square, top with the toasted marshmallow, and sandwich with another graham cracker.
3. Serve warm and enjoy!

Pudding Parfaits

Ingredients:

- 2 cups chocolate pudding (store-bought or homemade)
- 1 cup whipped cream
- Crumbled cookies (such as Oreos or graham crackers)
- Fresh berries for topping

Instructions:

1. In a glass, layer chocolate pudding, whipped cream, crumbled cookies, and fresh berries.
2. Repeat layers until the glass is filled.
3. Top with whipped cream and more berries.
4. Serve chilled.

Gelato

Ingredients:

- 2 cups whole milk
- 1 cup heavy cream
- 1 cup sugar
- 1 tablespoon vanilla extract

Instructions:

1. In a saucepan, heat milk and cream until warm, but not boiling.
2. In a separate bowl, whisk together sugar and vanilla.
3. Gradually whisk the sugar mixture into the warm milk and cream.
4. Cool the mixture to room temperature, then chill in the fridge for 2 hours.
5. Churn in an ice cream maker according to the manufacturer's instructions.
6. Freeze for an additional 2 hours before serving.

Coconut Cream Pie

Ingredients:

- 1 pre-baked pie crust
- 2 cups whole milk
- 1 cup heavy cream
- 3/4 cup sugar
- 3 tablespoons cornstarch
- 1/4 teaspoon salt
- 4 large egg yolks
- 1 teaspoon vanilla extract
- 1 cup shredded coconut

Instructions:

1. In a saucepan, combine milk, cream, sugar, cornstarch, and salt. Cook over medium heat, whisking constantly, until thickened.
2. Whisk a little hot mixture into egg yolks to temper them, then return to the saucepan and cook for 2 more minutes.
3. Remove from heat and stir in vanilla extract and shredded coconut.
4. Pour the filling into the pie crust and refrigerate for 4 hours.
5. Top with whipped cream and toasted coconut before serving.

Mocha Cake

Ingredients:

- 1 1/2 cups all-purpose flour
- 1 teaspoon baking powder
- 1/2 teaspoon baking soda
- 1/4 teaspoon salt
- 1/2 cup unsweetened cocoa powder
- 1 cup sugar
- 1/2 cup unsalted butter, softened
- 2 large eggs
- 1 teaspoon vanilla extract
- 1/2 cup brewed coffee
- 1/2 cup milk

Instructions:

1. Preheat the oven to 350°F (175°C). Grease and flour two 9-inch round cake pans.
2. In a bowl, whisk together flour, cocoa powder, baking powder, baking soda, and salt.
3. In another bowl, beat sugar and butter until creamy. Add eggs one at a time, then vanilla extract.
4. Add the dry ingredients alternately with coffee and milk, mixing until smooth.
5. Divide the batter between the two pans and bake for 25-30 minutes, or until a toothpick comes out clean.
6. Cool completely before frosting with mocha frosting or whipped cream.

Almond Joy Cake

Ingredients:

- 1 box chocolate cake mix
- 1/2 cup unsweetened cocoa powder
- 1/2 cup vegetable oil
- 3 eggs
- 1 cup buttermilk
- 1/2 cup coconut flakes
- 1 cup chopped almonds
- 1 cup mini marshmallows
- 1 cup chocolate frosting (store-bought or homemade)

Instructions:

1. Preheat the oven to 350°F (175°C). Grease and flour a 9x13-inch baking pan.
2. Prepare the chocolate cake mix according to package instructions, adding cocoa powder, vegetable oil, eggs, and buttermilk.
3. Fold in the coconut flakes, chopped almonds, and marshmallows.
4. Pour the batter into the prepared pan and bake for 30-35 minutes, or until a toothpick comes out clean.
5. Cool completely and frost with chocolate frosting.
6. Top with additional chopped almonds and coconut flakes.

Chocolate Fudge Cake

Ingredients:

- 1 box chocolate cake mix
- 1 cup sour cream
- 1/2 cup vegetable oil
- 3 eggs
- 1 teaspoon vanilla extract
- 1 cup chocolate chips
- 1/2 cup heavy cream
- 1/4 cup sugar

Instructions:

1. Preheat the oven to 350°F (175°C). Grease and flour a round cake pan.
2. Prepare the chocolate cake mix according to package instructions, adding sour cream, vegetable oil, eggs, and vanilla extract.
3. Stir in the chocolate chips.
4. Pour the batter into the pan and bake for 25-30 minutes, or until a toothpick comes out clean.
5. In a saucepan, heat heavy cream and sugar over medium heat until it begins to simmer. Remove from heat and stir in more chocolate chips until smooth.
6. Pour the fudge sauce over the cooled cake and serve.

Bananas Foster

Ingredients:

- 2 ripe bananas, sliced
- 1/4 cup butter
- 1/4 cup dark rum
- 1/2 cup brown sugar
- 1/2 teaspoon cinnamon
- 1/2 teaspoon vanilla extract
- Vanilla ice cream (for serving)

Instructions:

1. In a large skillet, melt butter over medium heat. Stir in brown sugar and cinnamon until the sugar has dissolved.
2. Add the sliced bananas to the skillet and cook for 2-3 minutes, until the bananas are soft.
3. Carefully add rum to the pan and ignite with a long lighter to flambé (optional but traditional). Allow the flames to subside.
4. Stir in vanilla extract and remove from heat.
5. Serve the bananas over a scoop of vanilla ice cream and pour the sauce over the top.

Sticky Toffee Pudding

Ingredients:

- 1 cup chopped dates
- 1 cup water
- 1 teaspoon baking soda
- 1/2 cup unsalted butter, softened
- 1/2 cup brown sugar
- 2 large eggs
- 1 teaspoon vanilla extract
- 1 1/2 cups all-purpose flour
- 1/2 teaspoon baking powder
- 1/4 teaspoon salt
- 1/2 cup heavy cream
- 1/4 cup dark brown sugar (for sauce)
- 1/4 cup unsalted butter (for sauce)

Instructions:

1. Preheat the oven to 350°F (175°C). Grease and flour a 9x9-inch baking pan.
2. In a saucepan, bring water and chopped dates to a boil, then remove from heat. Stir in baking soda and let sit for 5 minutes.
3. In a bowl, cream together butter and brown sugar. Beat in eggs and vanilla extract.
4. In a separate bowl, whisk together flour, baking powder, and salt. Gradually add the dry ingredients to the wet ingredients, alternating with the date mixture.
5. Pour the batter into the prepared pan and bake for 30-35 minutes, until a toothpick comes out clean.
6. For the sauce, melt butter in a saucepan, then stir in brown sugar and cream. Bring to a simmer for 3-4 minutes, stirring constantly.
7. Serve the sticky toffee pudding with the warm toffee sauce.

Fried Ice Cream

Ingredients:

- 4 scoops of vanilla ice cream
- 2 cups cornflakes, crushed
- 1 teaspoon cinnamon
- 1/4 cup sugar
- 1 egg, beaten
- Vegetable oil (for frying)
- Honey or chocolate sauce (for drizzling)

Instructions:

1. Scoop the ice cream into balls and freeze them for at least 1 hour to harden.
2. In a bowl, combine crushed cornflakes, cinnamon, and sugar.
3. Dip each ice cream ball into the beaten egg, then roll in the cornflake mixture until evenly coated.
4. Heat oil in a deep fryer or skillet to 375°F (190°C).
5. Fry the ice cream balls for 20-30 seconds, until golden and crispy.
6. Serve immediately, drizzled with honey or chocolate sauce.

Choco-Tacos

Ingredients:

- 6 taco shells (store-bought or homemade)
- 2 cups chocolate ice cream
- 1/2 cup mini chocolate chips
- 1/4 cup crushed nuts (optional)
- 1/2 cup hot fudge sauce

Instructions:

1. Freeze taco shells for 30 minutes to ensure they stay crispy when filled.
2. Scoop chocolate ice cream into each taco shell and gently press to shape it.
3. Sprinkle the ice cream with mini chocolate chips and crushed nuts (if using).
4. Drizzle hot fudge sauce over the ice cream.
5. Freeze the filled taco shells for another 30 minutes before serving.

Cheesecake Brownies

Ingredients:

- 1 box brownie mix (plus ingredients called for on the box)
- 8 oz cream cheese, softened
- 1/4 cup granulated sugar
- 1 egg
- 1 teaspoon vanilla extract

Instructions:

1. Preheat the oven according to the brownie mix instructions. Grease a 9x9-inch baking pan.
2. Prepare the brownie mix according to the package directions and pour the batter into the pan.
3. In a bowl, beat together cream cheese, sugar, egg, and vanilla extract until smooth.
4. Spoon the cream cheese mixture over the brownie batter and swirl with a knife to create a marble effect.
5. Bake according to brownie mix instructions, typically 25-30 minutes.
6. Cool before slicing into squares.

Fruit Tart

Ingredients:

- 1 pre-baked tart shell
- 1 cup vanilla pastry cream (store-bought or homemade)
- 1/2 cup fresh berries (strawberries, blueberries, raspberries, etc.)
- 1 tablespoon apricot jam (for glaze)

Instructions:

1. Fill the tart shell with vanilla pastry cream.
2. Arrange fresh berries on top of the cream in a decorative pattern.
3. In a small saucepan, heat apricot jam until melted. Brush the glaze over the fruit.
4. Chill the tart for at least 1 hour before serving.

Milkshakes

Ingredients:

- 2 cups vanilla ice cream
- 1/2 cup milk
- 1/4 cup chocolate syrup (optional)
- Whipped cream (optional)

Instructions:

1. Blend ice cream, milk, and chocolate syrup (if using) until smooth.
2. Pour into glasses and top with whipped cream.
3. Serve immediately with a straw.

Tarte Tatin

Ingredients:

- 6-8 apples, peeled and cored
- 1/2 cup unsalted butter
- 1 cup granulated sugar
- 1 sheet puff pastry
- 1 teaspoon vanilla extract

Instructions:

1. Preheat the oven to 375°F (190°C).
2. In a skillet, melt butter and sugar over medium heat, stirring until it forms a golden caramel.
3. Arrange the apples in a spiral pattern in the caramel and cook for 15 minutes, until the apples soften.
4. Remove from heat and place the puff pastry over the apples, tucking the edges into the pan.
5. Bake for 25-30 minutes, until the pastry is golden and puffed.
6. Let the tart cool for 5 minutes before inverting onto a serving plate.

Cupcakes

Ingredients:

- 1 box cake mix (or your favorite homemade recipe)
- 1/2 cup vegetable oil
- 3 eggs
- 1 cup water
- 1/2 cup butter, softened
- 4 cups powdered sugar
- 2 teaspoons vanilla extract

Instructions:

1. Preheat the oven to 350°F (175°C). Line a cupcake tin with paper liners.
2. Prepare the cake mix according to the package directions.
3. Fill each cupcake liner about 2/3 full with batter.
4. Bake for 18-20 minutes, or until a toothpick comes out clean.
5. Allow the cupcakes to cool completely before frosting.
6. For the frosting, beat butter until creamy, then gradually add powdered sugar and vanilla extract until smooth.
7. Frost the cupcakes and decorate with sprinkles or toppings of your choice.

Lemon Bars

Ingredients:

- **Crust:**
    - 1 1/2 cups all-purpose flour
    - 1/4 cup powdered sugar
    - 1/2 cup unsalted butter, cold and cubed
- **Filling:**
    - 1 1/4 cups granulated sugar
    - 2 tablespoons all-purpose flour
    - 4 large eggs
    - 1/2 cup fresh lemon juice
    - Zest of 1 lemon
    - Powdered sugar for dusting

Instructions:

1. Preheat the oven to 350°F (175°C). Grease a 9x9-inch baking dish.
2. For the crust, combine the flour and powdered sugar. Cut in the butter until the mixture resembles coarse crumbs.
3. Press the crust mixture into the bottom of the baking dish. Bake for 15 minutes or until lightly golden.
4. For the filling, whisk together sugar, flour, eggs, lemon juice, and lemon zest until smooth.
5. Pour the filling over the baked crust and return to the oven. Bake for 20-25 minutes, until set.
6. Let the bars cool completely. Dust with powdered sugar before serving.

Soufflé

Ingredients:

- 2 tablespoons unsalted butter
- 2 tablespoons all-purpose flour
- 1 cup whole milk, heated
- 1/2 cup grated cheese (optional for savory soufflés)
- 4 large eggs, separated
- 1/2 teaspoon vanilla extract (for dessert soufflé)
- 1/4 cup sugar (for dessert soufflé)
- Pinch of salt

Instructions:

1. Preheat the oven to 375°F (190°C). Butter and sugar (or flour) individual ramekins.
2. Melt butter in a saucepan, stir in flour, and cook for 1 minute to make a roux.
3. Gradually add heated milk to the roux, whisking constantly to avoid lumps. Cook until thickened.
4. Remove from heat and stir in egg yolks, vanilla extract (for dessert), cheese (for savory), and salt.
5. Beat egg whites with sugar until stiff peaks form. Gently fold the whites into the base mixture.
6. Pour the soufflé mixture into the prepared ramekins and bake for 20-25 minutes, or until golden and puffed.
7. Serve immediately, as soufflés deflate quickly.

Almond Cake

Ingredients:

- 1 cup almond flour
- 1/2 cup all-purpose flour
- 1 teaspoon baking powder
- 1/4 teaspoon salt
- 1/2 cup unsalted butter, softened
- 1 cup sugar
- 4 large eggs
- 1 teaspoon vanilla extract
- 1/2 cup milk

Instructions:

1. Preheat the oven to 350°F (175°C). Grease and flour a 9-inch round cake pan.
2. In a bowl, mix almond flour, all-purpose flour, baking powder, and salt.
3. In another bowl, cream together butter and sugar until fluffy. Beat in the eggs one at a time, then add vanilla extract.
4. Gradually add the dry ingredients and milk, mixing until smooth.
5. Pour the batter into the prepared pan and bake for 25-30 minutes, or until a toothpick comes out clean.
6. Cool completely before frosting or serving.

Strawberry Gelato

Ingredients:

- 2 cups fresh strawberries, hulled and chopped
- 3/4 cup granulated sugar
- 1 cup whole milk
- 1 cup heavy cream
- 1 teaspoon lemon juice

Instructions:

1. In a blender or food processor, puree the strawberries with 1/4 cup of sugar and lemon juice.
2. In a bowl, combine the strawberry puree with the remaining sugar, milk, and cream. Stir to dissolve the sugar.
3. Pour the mixture into an ice cream maker and churn according to the manufacturer's instructions.
4. Transfer to an airtight container and freeze for at least 2 hours before serving.

Cinnamon Rolls

Ingredients:

- **Dough:**
    - 2 1/4 teaspoons active dry yeast
    - 1/2 cup warm milk
    - 1/4 cup granulated sugar
    - 4 cups all-purpose flour
    - 1/2 teaspoon salt
    - 1/4 cup unsalted butter, softened
    - 2 large eggs
- **Filling:**
    - 1/2 cup unsalted butter, softened
    - 1 cup brown sugar
    - 2 tablespoons ground cinnamon
- **Icing:**
    - 1 cup powdered sugar
    - 2 tablespoons milk
    - 1/2 teaspoon vanilla extract

Instructions:

1. In a bowl, combine warm milk, sugar, and yeast. Let sit for 5 minutes until bubbly.
2. Add flour, salt, butter, and eggs to the yeast mixture. Knead until smooth and elastic. Let rise in a warm place for 1 hour.
3. Roll out the dough on a floured surface. Spread softened butter, brown sugar, and cinnamon evenly over the dough. Roll up tightly and slice into 12 rolls.
4. Place the rolls in a greased baking dish. Let rise for 30 minutes.
5. Preheat the oven to 350°F (175°C) and bake for 25-30 minutes, until golden brown.
6. For the icing, mix powdered sugar, milk, and vanilla. Drizzle over the warm rolls before serving.

Waffle Sundaes

Ingredients:

- 4 waffles (store-bought or homemade)
- 2 cups vanilla ice cream
- 1/2 cup chocolate sauce
- 1/2 cup whipped cream
- Chopped nuts (optional)
- Maraschino cherries (optional)

Instructions:

1. Toast the waffles according to your recipe or package instructions.
2. Place each waffle on a plate and top with a scoop of vanilla ice cream.
3. Drizzle with chocolate sauce and add whipped cream, nuts, and cherries.
4. Serve immediately and enjoy!

Nougat

Ingredients:

- 1 1/2 cups honey
- 1 cup sugar
- 1/4 cup water
- 2 egg whites
- 1/2 cup chopped nuts (almonds, pistachios, or hazelnuts)
- 1 teaspoon vanilla extract

Instructions:

1. In a saucepan, combine honey, sugar, and water. Bring to a boil over medium heat, stirring until sugar dissolves.
2. Cook until the mixture reaches 250°F (120°C) on a candy thermometer.
3. While the syrup is heating, beat egg whites to stiff peaks in a separate bowl.
4. Gradually pour the hot syrup into the egg whites, continuing to beat until the mixture thickens.
5. Stir in the nuts and vanilla extract.
6. Pour the nougat into a lined baking dish and let cool for 2-3 hours. Cut into squares.